# Contents

# 1

# Introduction

Personal content label content material will come in a number of forms. You will discover from eBooks, studies and posts, to complete "business in a box" packages including revenue web pages, direct magnets and even back-end merchandise.

The situation isn't in finding PLR. The difficulty is in understanding exactly how to earn money along with it in order to improve your revenue!

We have personally used exclusive label content material in several ways throughout the years, of course, if done properly, PLR can ultimately improve your earnings with almost no time and effort by you.

Before we start, it is crucial that you recognize that not every private brand content articles are made the same.

The important thing to earning cash with Private label rights is to find the finest quality content material probable. Afterwards you make basic tweaks and adjustments to the articles, and in the long run, you get a polished, market-prepared package deal that your consumers will gladly buy.

Personal content label content is amongst the simplest ways to produce a lot more content, which equates to more income.

After all, the greater number of information you may place available, the better it reaches attract sales opportunities, customers and clients. Content material power anything from marketing campaigns, account sites, to backend systems.

Regardless of whether you're a blog writer, affiliate internet marketer or creator, you need clean, targeted content that talks to your market and furthers your brand name.

The thing is, producing content material for the organization may be incredibly time-consuming. Positive, you can outsource it to specialist freelance writers, but when you're with a limited budget that isn't always a possibility.

Exclusive content label articles is a simple, inexpensive way to get this completed.

PLR allows you to take somebody else's production and brand it entirely for your very own.

Better yet, it is possible to cost it however you desire, make use of the content material in many different techniques, which include membership sites, weblogs and back-finish techniques.

It’s not merely among the most effective to maximize your revenue, but it is also one of many speediest ways to strike-start a new business, marketing campaign, or to try out the oceans in an unfamiliar niche market.

In this special record, you’ll learn about getting Private label rights articles from certified content material professionals, then selling that information with a better cost, although continuously increasing your profits funnel to ensure you’re capable to quickly increase your cash flow and set yourself up for long-term success.

Let’s get started!

# 2

# Understanding License Terms

Comprehending Permit Terms

Whenever you purchase individual tag content material, it is very vital that you completely comprehend the terms of your certification.

Even though Private label rights would be wise to feature the choice to change the information and include your business and company on the fabric, when it comes to syndication you can find sometimes constraints in position.

Understanding precisely what your certification allows you to do even before you start to take advantage of the content material is extremely important. You never ever would like to chance any possible legal issues by using Private label rights content material in a fashion that goes against the developer's phrases and certification limits.

Some of the things you need to pay close attention to when selecting exclusive label information incorporate:

Whether or not you are able to revise the content.

PLR should always provide you with the choice to customize the content material, include your own name, website link and also other branding information.

If you purchase content that doesn't permit adjustments, it's usually known as "Resale Rights" licensing, or "Master Resale Rights". Nonetheless, it's important to make certain, even though they supply you with the DOC/supply document.

Assert Authorship.

Exclusive label usually makes it possible for that this buyer to assert authorship, that means that one could put your own name about the information like you have been the first designer. Many other certification varieties, including RR (resell privileges), or MRR (grasp re-sell privileges) will not.

Exactly how the content can be used.

Never think that Private label rights information may be spread, sold and utilized in every way imaginable. Check your certificate for information on any syndication constraints (such as not being able to post on Amazon . com, or any other marketplaces), as well as any pricing limits.

Value Restrictions.

You may also want to pay attention to regardless of if the owner has set up a minimum price. Some vendors demand that you just do not promote the content below a set up minimal to protect the grade of the information. Even though this can't typically be forced officially, it's constantly a smart idea to keep to the seller's wishes. Should you don't similar to their certificate conditions, get another Private label rights vendor.

And speaking of accreditation, when you acquire Private label rights, it is recommended to be furnished with a complete, complete certificate that leaves nothing to guess work. Should you can't look for a license within your bundle, reach out to the designer and ask for a copy.

Only the very same, if you are ever baffled or doubtful about the regards to your license, have a min to make contact with the programmer before you start to work with the information.

Not every private content label content offers the identical licensing choices, so it is always important to validate with the creator just before making use of the substance.

For example, there are numerous forms of certification, which includes:

Individual (non-transferable) Personal Content label:

Using this type of license, you are typically capable to sell the content within your own manufacturer, however you are not permitted to move on those proper rights to other people.

Transferable Private Brand:

These certificates often let you successfully pass on personal brand proper rights to your clients.

Unhindered Individual Tag:

This kind of PLR certificate is considered the most adaptable, often allowing you to do whatever you desire together with the information.

Additionally, a number of Private label rights programmers will enable you to even give Private label rights apart, supplied within a account website instead of presented publically, when other designers don’t let the content to be offered apart, necessitating that it be sold.

# 3

# The price of PLR

Since you now much better comprehend the variation licenses often mounted on exclusive tag information, I wish to consider a closer inspection at the kind of exclusive tag articles that can make you the most money, and also PLR which is advisable to steer clear of.

To start, you must never acquire personal content label articles that comes with an “unrestricted” certificate.

An unhindered Private label rights license signifies you can do virtually nearly anything you want to do with the articles. You could potentially have aside, sell it, talk about PLR proper rights along with your clients, and distribute it openly and freely.

It is easy to understand what the problem is with this sort of certification, appropriate?

There is no benefit inside it!

You won't have the ability to convince people to acquire this sort of content material by you, if they're capable of finding it on countless other websites free of charge. There's no good quality manage in place. And that implies it is not proceeding that will help you further manufacturer consciousness, or perhaps be content that you'll desire to secure your business to. So, prevent unrestricted Private label rights whenever you can. There are actually far better certification options available.

Then again, the very best quality private label will only give you a constrained variety of PLR permits. Which means that you'll be certainly one of only a number of consumers to have a permit to work with this information. You won't handle an overload of competitors, or worry about your ability to sell this content because it won't be discovered freely on the web, or dispersed by 1000s of other dealers.

Whenever you can get a higher-good quality Private label rights creator supplying less than 100 permits, get a copy. This is the absolute greatest license you will find, and it'll be much better to promote this content and rebrand it as a your personal.

You also want to ensure that the PLR you purchase should not be presented out. It ought to always have to be offered. The only exception to this rule to this is where getting a direct magnet PLR deal.

Lead magnet Private label rights offers typically feature a entrance-finish report that people can use for an bonus to transform guests into clients.

While you still want to make certain that there are simply a limited number of permits available in order that there isn't an increased quantity of replicates in circulation, these Private label rights packages can be an easy way to setup steer internet pages quickly and easily.

As an example, https://promotelabs.com/alp-reseller/ gives you the opportunity to generate income reselling usage of refreshing new steer magnets each calendar month. People absolutely love these packages because they have private tag privileges, allowing them to adjust the information and employ it to convert guests into subscribers.

You can easily generate income by becoming a reseller of the website such as this, and better yet, you don't have to invest some time making a registration web site of your own simply because you simply direct your prospects to your very own join backlinks, they pay out straight, and then they are automatically redirected on the direct magnet download middle.

Regardless how you opt to monetize personal brand information, in relation to your certification legal rights, you wish to purchase PLR information that allows you to:

Market It (with individual proper rights only, non-transferable)

With these certification privileges, you will be able to sell private privileges for the completed product, and definitely will struggle to offer the content with individual content label legal rights to other people.

This is just what you want because you usually are not considering giving your clients the ability to move on the material to many other individuals, but rather, they may be purchasing a backup of a finished product for personal only use.

It will help to preserve the price of the item and sets you in greater control over circulation, while minimizing the amount of rivalry.

## Alter It

Most individual content label articles allows you to modify and revise the content nevertheless, you desire, including employing portions of the material to create much more information items.

In the next chapter, we will discuss a little more about ways to produce higher-high quality compilations from Private label rights that one could sell even for more money.

## Select Your Own Value Position

Several personal content label developers set a set selling price of what they presume their Private label rights product or service must be offered for. This is to safeguard the reliability in the product or service and to ensure that it retains its worth.

You would like to ensure that you are provided flexible legal rights with your Private label rights license to help you set your very own value on the product or service, not restricted to distinct value boundaries.

Market It as Your Very own (within your title)

Try not to get confused between Expert Reselling Rights and Exclusive Tag Rights. With Master Resale Privileges (called MRR), you happen to be rarely allowed to affect the content whatsoever, and they are not able to sell it off within your own label.

In reality, the main reason for MMR content articles are to present you a done item to sell, without needing to do any modifications or enhancements to the item.

Nevertheless, the downside to using Expert Reselling Privileges fabric is basically that you are promoting somebody else's manufacturer. As you can't change the content material, or put your company name in the material, (unless it's distributed as re-brandable information), you may be potentially funneling your prospects for the designer.

Think of this way: With individual label information, you might be protecting your supply of content from prying eye and competitors that want to know that you get the materials from.

With Grasp Resale Legal rights, your supply is visible, and even though it is possible to sell the merchandise, keeping 100% from the revenue, you will find it tough to build your own manufacturer.

# 4

# Making Profits With PLR

When choosing PLR, it is recommended to use a program set up for each and every deal you get. The most significant blunders that both new and seasoned marketers make when selecting Private label rights is within “over stocking”.

What occurs is that you end up buying excessive PLR at once without the real strategy concerning how you’ll use, or monetize it and eventually. Then, you end up with a hard disk packed with content material that you’ll never use. Or, once you end up formulating an agenda to the articles, it’s outdated and no longer popular!

So, start out with a straightforward strategy with a clear thought in your mind for every single Private label rights package deal you get. If you pick an eBook merchandise, consider adding it in as a added bonus object to further improve the value of another product, or if you buy some PLR reports, look at creating a collection which offers a whole-size tutorial plan.

A single fantastic way to earn money with PLR is to use compilations.

Here is how to get it done:

Gather up each of the PLR articles that you may have on specific issues, being sure that you stick to a style. The theory to make a total collection of goods within one market.

Compilations should have a number of Private label rights items that kind a group exercise program, so ensure that when you begin choosing goods for the collection, that every 1 works as a "module" that covers a specific place, and this with each other, you're capable to supply a complete training curriculum.

For instance, if you are considering building a compilation for the weight reduction industry, you might feature a number of records on weight loss tips, and perhaps an eBook on dieting, healthy ingesting and even Private label rights work out video clips.

One more case in point could possibly be with IM merchandise. You might easily develop a total-showcased "Social Advertising Course" that includes information about how to successfully market your organization in the distinct social websites stations by merely merging a number of PLR instructions on such things as Instagram, youtube and Pinterest.

Commence thinking of your first collection. What market market place are you enthusiastic about? What kind of content material would you like to come up with from PLR gives that will develop a completely-jam-packed education item?

Then, start looking on the web for high-high quality personal brand builders who offer you content material on those subject areas. Rebrand it as being your own with clean artwork, finished formatting, and create a complete-range, thorough package deal!

# 5

# Make Alluring Additional bonuses

Bonus products improve the recognized importance of items and comes out, which is why you've most likely seen that the majority of the sizeable-scale item launches provide a package of these.

Associates likewise use rewards to attract potential clients into acquiring through their internet affiliate website link instead of someone else's. This is just one simple way which you can use PLR information to increase your income!

Think about purchasing PLR that forms an auxiliary element to a key merchandise launch's total concept or subject matter, then offer it to customers who purchase from you.

For instance, if you are planning to promote an item kick off on running a blog, you can buy a number of PLR substance starting from WordPress styles to pre-filled articles or content and present it as a a benefit-boosted benefit for anybody who acquisitions via your website link!

Added bonus delivers would be wise to tie in directly with what’s on offer and present obvious value. Actually, your bonus provide must always include a “value price” connected with it, to ensure that potential customers know specifically what the added bonus will be worth, and what amount of cash they could save by getting through your affiliate marketer link.

It is possible to setup added bonus offers by making an account at https://commissiongorilla.com/v2/

Commission payment Gorilla will give you usage of an entire catalogue of reward items to select from so that you can quickly generate and help save an infinite amount of additional bonuses. That way, they are always prepared to help you if you want them. Give it a look.

# 6

# Generate High Ticket Info Merchandise

Surprisingly, you can even use exclusive content label content as being the central base for the items.

Although you should tweak and improve the merchandise so they fit your personal type and represent your brand, there is no reasons why you can't use PLR because the groundwork in which to build several great-stop info products.

The objective is going to be very distinct with the kind of PLR you get. Focus on credible PLR designers who supply continuing assistance, and who retain the services of only seasoned freelancers who can generate shiny, relevant and workable content.

The larger the expertise of the content material, the much less work will be involved in tweaking or enhancing it, so keep this in mind in choosing your private tag articles. And again, only buy individual content label content from builders who market just a limited number of permits. Doing this, you may be one of just one or two who can access this content material.

Quite often, you should expect to pay a lot more for high quality!

Consequently when you see PLR offered for $5, odds are, the material is of poor quality, or lower value for the reason that creator will have to promote a great deal of certificates to make up for the low price. So, bear that in mind while searching for private brand content material.

Give attention to only the quality of this content, and don’t concern yourself with everything else.

It is wise to repackage PLR by working with a fashionable to make new artwork that suit your manufacturer rather than utilize the artwork which come with the material (and therefore are likely utilized by other entrepreneurs). So, be aware of the content and don’t be worried about the “wrapping”.

If the standard of the material is solid, grab a certificate, touch within the articles, file format it, add your visuals and then sell it!

# 7

# Checklist Building With Private label rights

Personal label content articles are also extremely beneficial at starting to warm up customers (pre-promoting), in addition to developing and monetizing a subscriber list.

In e-mail marketing, one of the more important components is within offering regular upgrades and value to subscribers. It's also one of many only methods to preserve members in addition to construct useful partnerships with those on the listing.

So, use private tag content material to strength the e-mail lists!

This can be done by splitting apart report content, or writing PLR information as articles or content and then notifying your databases of your recent up-date and directing them to your site.

You can also use PLR reports and EBooks as bonus delivers on your own squash pages, to tempt guests into being members.

Further more, you may use Private label rights to offer typical, regular followup emails which contain pre-composed autoresponder messages, enabling you to place your email marketing on complete autopilot!

In case you have Private label rights content that particulars one step-by-phase process, or a series of associated suggestions, then you can easily transform this articles right into a multiple-part e-course.

In case you have an adequate amount of this content, you can even create an email sequence that runs completely automatically for three months, a few months, annually or even more! (and don't overlook, online video content material is very rewarding with this to – just deliver your clients a video hyperlink in addition to the email messages and drive website traffic back to your blog!)

You have to give your possible clients a good reason to join your subscriber list. One method to accomplish that is by supplying a freebie that holders outside the rest.

While many entrepreneurs are satisfied to offer you cost-free studies or eBooks you can take in sales opportunities with great online video content material that prospective subscribers place a much greater importance on)

If you're seeking substantial-quality PLR list constructing information you could rebrand as the own and start making use of to create and energy your email lists, you'll want to have a look at: https://promotelabs.com/provides/leadpack-offer you/ where you could grab 6 done-for-you steer magnets, complete with personal label proper rights.

# 8

# Develop Registration Sites

Yet another incredibly potent strategy for earning money with individual tag content articles are with account websites. Continuity sites are incredibly profitable because instead of having a customer as soon as, you build a group where members buy accessibility every 30 days.

It is possible to set this tactic for the analyze in a few different methods, which includes by building a Private label rights membership site that simply capabilities new PLR and RR goods weekly. So, you essentially situation yourself as being a Private label rights supplier.

All you have to do is join a Private label rights account web site that permits you to re-sell the content. Then, include that substance to your individual membership site and demand anywhere between $10-30 per month!

A good example of a regular membership site which offers high quality Private label rights content material that you might use within your continuity program is: http://www.SurefireWealth.com

Guaranteed Wealth has existed for a number of many years, and yes it continues to keep an integral resource for quality articles and emits. The highest point about Straightforward Wealth is that you may also access a total library of training substance and manuals totally free simply by browsing their website.

If you wish unhindered use of their total inventory of training substance as well as plenty of high quality personal tag content material, it is possible to become a member of being a paid out participant.

And also as we've discussed earlier, you may create your very own original content packages depending on Private label rights compilations. Each and every month, you can use Private label rights to maintain your web site up-to-date.

Then, make your individual membership coaching center and give this content each and every month in your associates! When you aren't certain how to setup a regular membership internet site, have a look at http://www.ProductDyno.com

Item Dyno is probably the easiest ways to construct a continuity website without having to mount program code or fool around with scripts and complex layouts.

No matter what your niche, your regular membership web site must always have a style. So, if you're enthusiastic about a niche like "Weight Loss", everything, instruments and assets within your account website ought to be focused with that certain matter. If you would like branch out, make more membership web sites that will develop a lucrative network.

Private label rights can potential as several membership websites as you may treatment to build!

# 9

# Closing Terms

Here are a few other methods to start earning money with exclusive content label information:

Develop a paid merchandise with PLR content material.

You may reserve your best PLR content and employ it to produce paid for goods, including fixed word memberships, bodily merchandise/residence study courses, paid webinars plus more.

Tip: For optimum outcomes, put together multiple resources for PLR to generate your very own special, killer item.

Use PLR content to create a viral report.

Do you possess PLR information that seems particularly useful, engaging, entertaining as well as better, debatable? Then apply it to produce a popular report that you spread widely across your area of interest to usher in a boost in traffic to the internet site.

Convert textual content PLR articles in to a video

Never restrict yourself to trying to keep your PLR content material in the initial textual content formatting. A great way to expand its use is usually to convert written text articles into video content. Then, add to websites like Vimeo.com and YouTube.com and push in clean, targeted traffic.

Compile PLR articles to make a “vault” account internet site

Have you got a lot of PLR content all in one market? Then apply it to create a vault-fashion account internet site, that is chock-loaded with video clips, market articles, reviews & eBooks. Demand a one-time fee for admittance and provide account into the income funnels being a short time supply.

Or build a free registration website as a way to create prospects and build a consumer collection!

Post PLR content material on your own weblog

Should you do not possess PLR posts, no concerns – you are able to draw out PLR from studies and e books to instantly make quick blog articles! Compile information from numerous sources to generate a full-highlighted post that may be reveal-deserving.

Produce a podcast out from PLR information

Instead of posting typical text message content on the website or Facebook wall structure, you may take the mp3 from videos to create a podcast. On top of that, after that you can submit this podcast to podcast internet directories and connect with new prospects and customers!

I have offered you many different suggestions with regards to how you can begin to use personal brand content to construct your business and optimize your cash flow. The next step should be to get the very best quality content material possible, as well as develop a strategy for every package you buy.

To your achievement!

# 10

# Resources

Here are links to the resources found in this guide:

**Commission Gorilla:**

**http://www.CommissionGorilla.com**

Gain instant access to a full library of bonus products to choose from so that you can quickly create and save an unlimited number of bonuses. That way, they're always ready for you to use when you need them.

**Product Dyno:**

**http://www.ProductDyno.com**

The easiest way to set up a digital content storefront online quickly while automating the delivery of your product. Very easy to set up and use if you wish to minimize your workload and streamline your product launch.

**Lead Magnet Pack**

**https://promotelabs.com/offers/leadpack-offer/**

Grab your license to 6 done-for-you lead magnets that include everything you need to build a mailing list.

**Surefire Wealth**

**http://www.SurefireWealth.com**

Gain instant access to thousands of PLR, MRR and RR products, along with free training videos and more.

**Promote Labs**

**https://promotelabs.com/offers/**

For additional PLR offers that you can rebrand as your own, check out

PromoteLabs.com for fresh, new white label packages and more.

www.ingramcontent.com/pod-product-compliance
Lightning Source LLC
LaVergne TN
LVHW041306150826
845673LV00008B/2754

* 9 7 9 8 4 6 1 0 5 7 7 1 8 *